# Cute Stuff

by Lucy McClymont
illustrations by Cary Pillo Lassen

**Harcourt Brace & Company**
Orlando Atlanta Austin Boston San Francisco Chicago Dallas New York Toronto London

“I’m taking the mule to
Yuletown,” Bule said.

"Get stuff we can USE!"
Bule's wife said.

"We use fuses," Bule said.

Bule got fuses.

"What cute cubes!" Bule said. "We could use cubes!"

"What cute ukes!" Bule said. "We could use ukes!"

"Will this fit on the mule?" Bule asked.

Bule put the fuses in the ukes, the ukes in the cubes, and the cubes on the mule.

"Fuses?" asked Bule's wife.

Bule took the cubes off the mule, the ukes out of the cubes, and the fuses out of the ukes.

“Fuses!” Bule said. “And some cute stuff we can use!”